THE SCARIEST PLACES ON EARTH

TOWER OF LONDON

BY DENNY VON FINN

BELLWETHER MEDIA · MINNEAPOLIS, MN

Are you ready to take it to the extreme?
Torque books thrust you into the action-packed world
of sports, vehicles, mystery, and adventure. These
books may include dirt, smoke, fire, and chilling tales.
WARNING : read at your own risk.

Library of Congress Cataloging-in-Publication Data

Von Finn, Denny.
 Tower of London / by Denny Von Finn.
    pages cm. -- (Torque : the scariest places on earth)
 Includes bibliographical references and index.
 Summary: "Engaging images accompany information about the Tower of London. The combination
of high-interest subject matter and light text is intended for students in grades 3 through 7"--Provided by
publisher.
 ISBN 978-1-60014-951-1 (hardcover : alk. paper)
 1. Haunted prisons--England--London--Juvenile literature. 2. Ghosts--England--London--Juvenile
literature. 3. Tower of London (London, England)--Miscellanea--Juvenile literature. 4. Tower of London
(London, England)--History--Juvenile literature. I. Title.
 BF1477.3.V66 2014
 133.1'294215--dc23
                                                                    2013009613

This edition first published in 2014 by Bellwether Media, Inc.

Printed in the United States of America, North Mankato, MN.

TABLE OF CONTENTS

CHAPTER 1

LOST AT THE TOWER OF LONDON

A cold, wet fog is rolling off the River Thames. The sun has begun to set in the October sky. You have spent the day exploring the Tower of London. Now it is about to close for the night. Suddenly, you notice that you have wandered from your group.

WINGED GUARDIANS

Six ravens are kept on the Tower of London grounds at all times. It is believed that the Tower and United Kingdom will fall if its ravens ever leave.

Startled, you look around. Not a soul in sight! Where did they go? A raven caws from a bare branch above. You quickly set off down the wet cobblestones. Were those footsteps? You spin around. Your heart leaps. A ghostly white **apparition** is following you. And it has no head!

CHAPTER 2
A BLOODY PAST

The Tower of London is a castle with 21 towers. It gets its name from the White Tower. This was the first of the castle's many buildings. The White Tower was completed around 1100. The Tower of London grew over the years. It was a home for royalty. It also served as a prison.

CROWN JEWELS

England's greatest treasures are called the Crown Jewels. They are kept in a heavily guarded building at the Tower of London.

White Tower

It is no surprise that the Tower of London is one of England's most haunted places. It was a site of **torture** and **execution** for hundreds of years. Criminals, spies, and even queens were killed there. Their moaning ghosts have floated through the Tower ever since.

The heads of those executed at the Tower of London were often displayed on tall stakes for others to see.

CHAPTER 3

GHOSTS OF THE TOWER

The Tower of London's most famous ghost is that of Anne Boleyn. Anne was the Queen of England from 1533 to 1536. Her husband was King Henry VIII. He declared her a **traitor** and had her **beheaded**.

Anne Boleyn

Many **Yeoman Warders** have seen
Anne's ghost over the years. In 1864,
a guard met her headless figure. He
stabbed it with his **bayonet**, but the
ghost passed right through. The guard
fainted from fright.

The Princes in the Tower are also famous ghosts. Princes Edward and Richard were just 12 and 9 years old when they disappeared in 1483.

Many believe the boys' uncle had them killed when he became king. He was afraid they would take his throne. In 1674, workers found the bones of two children buried under a stairway.

The tower in which the princes lived became known as the Bloody Tower. Once, the daughter of a Yeoman Warder who lived there found the princes sitting on her bed. Her parents rushed to her room when they heard her scream. The princes were gone, but the room was damp and chilly.

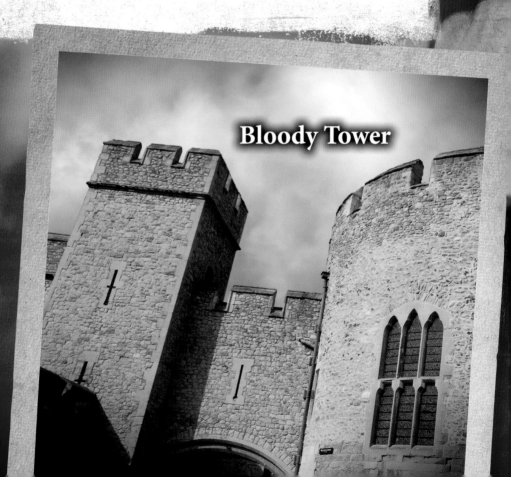

Bloody Tower

King Edward

17

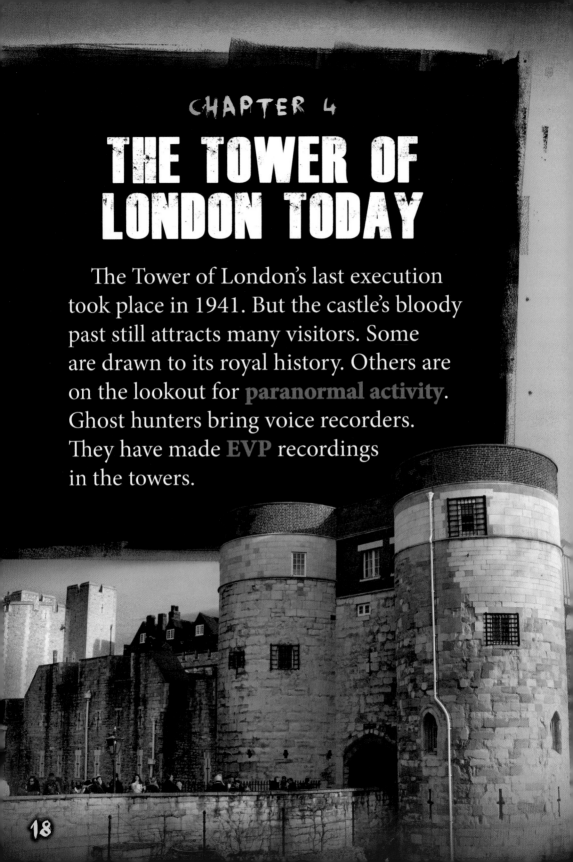

CHAPTER 4

THE TOWER OF LONDON TODAY

The Tower of London's last execution took place in 1941. But the castle's bloody past still attracts many visitors. Some are drawn to its royal history. Others are on the lookout for **paranormal activity**. Ghost hunters bring voice recorders. They have made **EVP** recordings in the towers.

THE GHOST OF MARGARET POLE

Margaret Pole was sentenced to beheading in 1541. The executioner's first swing missed her neck and hit her shoulder. Margaret tried to run, but the executioner chased her down. Their ghosts are said

Many prisoners arrived at the Tower of London through Traitor's Gate on the River Thames. Visitors today can imagine passing through here in a boat, never to be free again.

It has been a long time since prisoners were tortured and killed at the Tower of London. But their ghosts still haunt the castle as they relive their pain forever. Visit someday and maybe they will share it with you!

Traitor's Gate

GLOSSARY

apparition—a ghostly figure

bayonet—a sharp blade attached to the end of a gun

beheaded—killed by having one's head chopped off

EVP—electronic voice phenomena; EVP recordings sound like speech but have no known source.

execution—the killing of prisoners as punishment for crimes

paranormal activity—strange events with no known explanation

royalty—the kings, queens, princes, or princesses who rule some countries

torture—the act of forcing someone to suffer extreme pain

traitor—a person who turns against another

Yeoman Warders—the guards and tour guides of the Tower of London

TO LEARN MORE

AT THE LIBRARY

Chandler, Matt. *The World's Most Haunted Places*. Mankato, Minn.: Capstone Press, 2012.

Riley, Gail Blasser. *Tower of London: England's Ghostly Castle*. New York, N.Y.: Bearport Pub., 2007.

Stone, Adam. *Ghosts*. Minneapolis, Minn.: Bellwether Media, 2011.

ON THE WEB

Learning more about the Tower of London is as easy as 1, 2, 3.

1. Go to www.factsurfer.com.

2. Enter "Tower of London" into the search box.

3. Click the "Surf" button and you will see a list of related Web sites.

With factsurfer.com, finding more information is just a click away.

INDEX

The images in this book are reproduced through the courtesy of: Giancario Liguori, front cover (top); Javier Larrea/ Age Fotostock, front cover (bottom); Croisy, front cover & p. 20 (skull); Justin Black, pp. 2-3 (background); Tetra Images/ SuperStock, pp. 4-5 (background); Petr Malyshev, pp. 6 (background), 13 (background); Kiselev Andrey Valerevich, pp. 6 (ghost), 13 (ghost); Gary J. Toth, p. 7; Mary Evans Picture Library/ Alamy, p. 8; Euroluftbild de/ F1 Online/ SuperStock, p. 9; The Print Collector/ Alamy, p. 10; Peter Casolino/ Alamy, p. 11; Classic Image/ Alamy, pp. 12, 14; Byggarn.se, p. 16; Hippolyte Delaroche/ Getty Images, p. 17; Dynamosquito/ Creative Commons, p. 18; INTERFOTO/ Alamy, p. 19; Phil King, p. 20; Samot, p. 21.